Falling: Love-Struck: The God Poems

by

Sophy Burnham

Finishing Line Press
Georgetown, Kentucky

Falling: Love-Struck:
The God Poems

Publisher: Leah Maines

Editor: Christen Kincaid

Cover Art: Sophy Burnham

Author Photo: Erin Kelleher

Cover Design: Elizabeth Maines

Printed in the USA on acid-free paper.
Order online: www.finishinglinepress.com
                also available on amazon.com

Author inquiries and mail orders:
Finishing Line Press
P. O. Box 1626
Georgetown, Kentucky 40324
U. S. A.

Table of Contents

Also by Sophy Burnham

Nonfiction
> The Art Crowd
> The Landed Gentry: Passions and Personalities Inside
>> America's Propertied Class
> A Book of Angels: Reflections on Angels Past & Present and
>> True Stories of How They Touch Our Lives
> Angel Letters
> The Ecstatic Journey: Walking the Mystical Path in
>> Everyday Life
> The Path of Prayer
> For Writers Only
> The Art of Intuition

Novels
> Revelations
> The President's Angel
> The Treasure of Montségur
> Buccaneer
> The Dogwalker

Plays
> Penelope: The Story of the Odyssey from her point of view
> Snowstorms (The Study)
> Prometheus: by Aeschylus, with new Conclusion
> The Meaning of Life

Children's Radio Plays (NPR)
> The Witch's Tale
> The Nightingale
> Beauty and the Beast

Preface

In my thirties and for many years, I prayed, confused and filled with inchoate longing, to know if there was God: "Show me! Show me!"

Then at forty-two a mystical revelation crashed over me[1], sudden, overwhelming, violent, majestic, terrible and magnificent, and I think that for the next twenty years my feet hardly touched the earth. (In other words I was quite ungrounded.) Some of the poems in this collection come from this period, when I was so caught up in the spiritual that I hardly noticed the physical world around me.

Later, as the visions and mystical experiences slowly faded, I found myself once more in the material world, but everything was changed, for now I saw God everywhere, in everything: the Suchness shining, until even what we call "evil" seems filled with a heart-stopping awareness of the Good. "Oh, Earth," says Emily in the play *Our Town*, "you're too wonderful for anyone to realize you." As earlier I had stood dazzled by the Numinous, I now found God-ness (so to speak) in the everyday daily-ness of ordinary things. The perspicacious reader will detect which of the poems in this collection come from the earlier and which from later periods.

Yes, I still sometimes see angels in the spaces between the branches of the trees, and often I see the people haloed by their energy field or aura. It takes my breath away—God shining, singing, pouring out love extravagantly, in every form and being.

---

[1] It is described in my book, *The Ecstatic Journey: Walking the Mystical Path in Everyday Life.*

Some people may wonder at calling these god-poems. Why is a light-hearted spoof of Robert Frost a "God-poem? How does recognition of the loss of words that comes with aging have anything to do with it? Somehow (and this is hard to explain), I'm overwhelmed by the rightness of life, of death, of aging, of the tremors of fear and anxiety that shake and unseat us. I see, to paraphrase Rilke, how rich is life, how just, how inexorable. How good it is, all of it, including that blind death toward which we are hiking from our first intake of breath and which makes life so dear. Oh, it's wonder-full.

Even in grief, we find a senseless joy reverberating, resonating underneath the tears. I wonder if God is not participating in all the suffering and pain of this physical plane, the losses, recognition, beauty, the sheer pleasure of having eyes to see with, tongues to taste with, hands for working tools, and arms to embrace each other with. I think again of Rilke. "What will you do, God, when I die?" In those years when I prayed with such anguish, "Oh, God, if there is a God, show yourself!" I would not have expected the answer to offer simply what's around. Until recently, I have never dared to show my poems to anyone, and so none have been published before.

Many people need to be acknowledged, for nothing is ever done all by oneself. I name especially my editor Jean Zimmer, and to Kathleen Stuardt, who encouraged me, and to all the staff at Finishing Line Press, including Christen Kincaid, and to my children Molly and Sarah, who praised and applauded when I was discouraged, and to Mary Doub and to my sister Anne, who read some of my poems and even made corrections, and especially who didn't hoot with derisive laughter—to everyone, I feel deeply in debt.

To a powerful politician

One day I saw a stranger's soul
When he came riding on a horse.
He made it pirouette in gold caparison,
Prance out bold deeds, strike sparks for my delight,
Brag proclamations of his might,
Drum thunder from the height.

But I was taken by an air instead
So soft he did not know it hovered near,
A tendril, valiant in its yearning how to grow,
A wisp of breath, a bleeding wonderment,
A hurt, a dear intent,
Its fragile strength unspent.

He thought it due his mastery, control, his huntsman's seat,
When I knelt marveling at his horse's feet.

I have seen the earth

I have seen the earth
Shining
      Flashing with light divine
But more wondrous is this:
     To observe
     With awe
Just common grime.

The basement stair

There was a day when I, a little child,
Was dancing in the sunbeam's shaft that filed
Or streamed across the chambered hallways of my mind
(I was all joy; no worlds were left to find)
And, laughing, whirled in rhythm with the luminous floats—
The spirit-lights like golden notes
Singing in the high air.
"What are you doing on the basement stair?"
It was my mother's voice. "How dare you? Just in underpants
And playing in the dust! You feel enhanced,
I s'pose, to be here smeared in dirt!"
She muttered more. I rose protesting pride against my hurt,
And still she would not stop. "I've never seen the like!"
I felt tears back against the dike
Of my control, then overflow, broken on her reproof.
I dressed. She stood aloof.
And then I saw the lights were only motes,
Gray dirt or grime against the cellar door, the kind of grit that floats
In any moldy air. The sun was gone.
So, too, the siren song.
It happened long ago, but oh! What I would give
To hear that song again and like a child sieve
Dancing sunlight out of golden beams,
In dirt stand dazzled at God's dreams.

I am a river

I am a river flowing to the sea.
I am the sky tossed over fields,
the very canopy
that trees—who are also me—
hold up with dazzled fingers, frayed and tasseled shields.

I am your thoughts,
a tapeworm curled inside,
unwinding all your life
in kaleidoscopic strife,
flowing to the sea,

which is also me.

What is the soul of my heart's love?

What is the soul of my heart's love?
A pearl
Glowing.

When I write

When I write I sometimes learn what it is I need to know
the way a dream will tell me sometimes
what I'm battling or need:

And now? Just be, it says. Be still.
Trust. Wait,
it says, connect—and breathe.

Drop into the golden light of patience,
Force nothing, as I'm trying to force the patterns now
without knowing the end or even what it is I want to say.

Water

Taking the easy path as it takes on the color of
Pebble bedded bottom brown
And flowing at a steady run downhill,
Trilling
Over stones it laughs as light as air until
Suddenly we see, in its dark pools of quiet optimism,
That it gives all back again:

The vaulting sky for miles deep down
And spun glass clouds
And trees
Shuddering as they hold the whole in place
With shimmering kisses to green winds.

Why does it never run against the slope?
It forces nothing, nor shouts,
Nor flexing muscles makes
Pronouncements of ambitious drive;
Only flows like the skin of a cat
Easy
And unresistant.
But in a million muttering years
It bends all to it path,
Melts rock, carves cliffs, sweeps out soil
Humming at its play
The easy way
No strain
No aim

If I were to write a love poem to my beloved

If I were to write a love poem to my Beloved
What words could come to show the Grace?
        My joy! My all!
My heart is melting in the fire of his gaze
While words fall grey and cold—dry ash.

Who can see the wind?
Known only by the veils of snow
        Blown white across white fields
Or in the silver quivering of leaves
        A shudder of delight—
        Like that of a girl locked in her lover's embrace
        When whispered breath blows kisses in her hair.

Who can smell the hum of honey bees
Or taste the violent yellow of Fall cottonwoods?

My Beloved comes.
Sometimes in the darkness of black night
        I hear the silent radiance of His approach
And run then to the welcoming door
Throw wide the wood, and if I'm swift
I see the bending of the shining grass
        Beneath His sandaled step,
And everything is bowing before that gaze
And everything is shining with sheer praise.

Belief

I can't believe it snowed again last night
I mean look at it,
The white fire dazzling my eyes
Against the blue cup of sky
The scent of wind-whipped snow
Stinging my skin.

I can't believe he didn't propose
After all that!
Three years of sleeping together
And feeding him and picking up his dirty
Socks. And then he packed
And left.

I can't believe the lousy dinner she served
When everyone knows she's rich as Croesus,
And not a drop of wine,
Because she's on the wagon,
She says, and if you believe that you believe
Anything.

I can't believe the radiation levels in Japan
Or the earthquake right on the heels of
Mudslides, drought, tornadoes, floods, more war.
For that matter I can't believe we're actually at war again
In some desert halfway round the world
And the financial meltdown: how much
I lost! Eeooooweee!
You wouldn't believe it.

But as for God, come on hey, give me a break,
It's like rational, I mean
Intellectual. Who
Can believe in God?

Bells! Bells!

My soul is the silence

of a bell

ringing.

Words, words

1. I'm losing my words
Or my mind, one or the other,
Groping for a name, a noun.
The adjective that used to
Leap like a young goat
Off
The cliffs of joy
Onto the page is
Now a stuttered shadow
Of a memory.
They come back, the words return
Drunk and reeling after a night at the bars.
They lurch into the empty streets,
bottle-swinging, shout: *Adjacent!*
Tapas! Ecru!
Daisy Miller!
Awake in bed I grind my teeth
Helpless against the green glass
Shattering on the dawn curbs
Curfew! Origami!
When what I needed was now hours gone.
They slink off laughing like felons
On the prowl.

2. I dream how when I die the words will all come back
Falling in apple blossom blessings
Paper whirligigs
Floating, falling through the silence
Majestically
White cranes curving
To my tongue
Taut and tangy to the touch.
They'll flap one indolent wing
To keep aloft
Swoop, settle on my scorchéd skin
Like burning kisses:
Affectionate, disorderly, extravagant
All the polysyllabic Latinates commingling
With rough Saxon sounds
As brash and coarse as crows.
They trudge through the forests of our history
Swords swinging, hacking out ransom,
wreck, match, milk, muck, reek,
crackle and *ax, barn* and *cairn.*
They are homey and redolent with the smell of dirt
or death. And we find
Chinese, Spanish, Arabic,
Yiddish, each word
Attesting to the endless
Migrations of humankind.

3. In my dream the words snow
Silently from gunmetal skies, drift in piles
And twirl light wind-whipped powder-soft,
These carriers of the fierce music
Of my life.
Buckled and booted for war
The huntsman's horn, the screech of wheel,
Laments of loneliness and love.
They are choral bells pealing forth their
Hope faith fears.
They are canticles to
The times
We've known before
This time round.
In my dream
I wonder if it's words I'll miss
The most
When I depart
Or whether words will wing
In whatever heaven I'm assigned.
I'd even want another incarnation
Here if I could hear
Words tumbling from your
Beautiful sweet mouth, pouring
From the bellows of your throat.

What is so patient

What is so soothing or so patient
As a white horse grazing
Thick neck down
And tail swishing at the idle flies
Its four hooves pinioned to the green?
The quiet intensity
Of cropping grass.

In the stillness of approaching dusk
The light turns golden; dogs hold their breath.
From far away a woodpecker batters at a tree
And stops.
The mourning dove calls its three-beat who-who-who
While insects hail the softening darkness with a high thin whine.
But nothing holds the stillness like the waiting trees
Whose roots spread in the dark soil
As wide as their umbrellad foliage
And tap the depths in echo of the sky-stroked heights:
The skin of Earth marks antimatter for a tree:
In light above, so deep in dark below.
A bumble bee hums against the screen,
A crow; the click and chirrup of an unknown bird.

We call it silence, this stillness before the coming dark.
But the trees know.
Slow down they say
Sit still
How can you see…
Anything…
When you can't
Be… quiet
For… a
Century…
Or two?

Skin

I think sometimes late at night
As I am floating down the stream of sleep
How if I had no skin
I would spill out of my body
Red heart still beating on the pavement—
    A lobster without its shell
The white muscles languishing idle and stringy as the tendons
They no longer tug.

Would the bones collapse clattering to the ground
    Like sticks
Had I no skin?
The giant splash of blood is
    of course
The most dramatic—buckets of blood
    landing splat
    on the sidewalk
Where only moments before perhaps
I stood admiring the lacy limbs of winter trees:
That splatter is the part
That nicks the neighbors, makes strangers
    leap back
    in startlement,
Although probably, now I think about it,
The blood would still be held
    in the blue veins, pulsing and pounding
Along the tangle of red arteries
    that wobble here and there, distressed,
    as if lost and searching for
Their safe warm barn with its sweet scent of hay, and the grains
Piled in mangers, and the soft munching of animals satisfied.

Drinking blood

Walking along the banks of the river
in a dream, it came to him
that we might drink water—*think*!
instead of blood:

An insight equal to that of Abraham these thousands of long years gone,
about slaughtering our own sons,
though we haven't done such a good job of it, have we?
sending them to war and handing out the knives
of sacrifice.

It must be part of human nature to drink blood.
Consider the news.
Count gunshot wounds, the bombs, the rough
and tumble of everyday time's turmoil, the quarrelling,
with each side insisting
on the right to claim right

passionately. Violence charges
into our privacy, exuberant. It filters
through air, intruding even on my telephone.

I think it wise therefore to keep a fast
on news, lest horror cast
so bleak a net we can't unhook our feet from
tangled and despairing seines.

Remember, children, goodness springs
up ever, always, constantly,
as shown by the tears that fill our
eyes this moment, reading what the Paper flings
at our door right now.

Pondering: Separate.

Once when I was so small I could hear the whisper of trees, the roar of rocks, green singing of the grass, when I knew what our dogs were thinking and where the cat wandered when she slithered out at night, then nothing could hurt me except the separating from the whole: Which felt impossible.

Onward I grew into a long-legged colt, whisking my tail as I bolted up the hills and by the time I reached my 15th conscious year, I suddenly realized I felt no belonging anymore but only anguish, having lost the wild upreaching climbing clawing beansprouts, the reddening strawberries hiding in the fields, the forest-floor of spongy moss that, thoughtless, I'd just trodden on, smashing the branches of those towering miniature trees.

And now I'm old again, or maybe young. Now I can sit in memory on the bank of that stream and consider the things that shiver beneath the trees of infinitesimal moss, ponder how strange it is that our planet should fly endlessly through space, eternally looping round a fiery star that is one of billions upon billions that sweep at unimaginable speed through space so vast and empty that all the burning stars and planets and comets, moons and other debris are like grains of sand scattered before the emptiness of that indifferent silence.

I think how much a part of it I am, how small (but large in my own self-centered skin). I think how Time now breathes me in and out, swallows and spills me into further worlds—and that will happen, yes, until I'm nothing but a particle of light, an element, a flicker perhaps of consciousness, and then the question comes: Will I feel a part of Something More? Be awestruck, marveling as before in passionate innocence? Or will I dissolve into the eternal pool, unseparate?

Creation

Listen.
Do you hear the
Twittering of that bird outside,
Fluttering,
A straw in her beak,
Intent on fashioning one by one
With twig, stick, down, hair, horse's tail,
A nest so intricate you can't imagine
Weaving it with fingers
Much less a tiny pointed yellow beak?

Creation foams forth
Prodigious. It forces itself in your face.
No getting around it: it's
What we're born to do
Whether we want to
Or not; and I think the eye of
God is loving our terrified attempts
To run hide flee, that finger hooked at us,
And calling: Come! Create!
Make
Something never seen before,
Make
Something strong true new

And give it beauty, too,
Because that's also needed
To survive.

One breath

Be still and
breathe. Is anything more important
than this (one breath)? You'd think
we'd think about it
      more,
The way we do when
pushed under
      water,
held down by your
bullying older brother in rough-
house joy, except
      you're thrashing flailing
gasping—oh god! For
      air
clear lovely and invisible sustenance
sucked greedy into collapsing lungs, the way
the asthmatic hauls in
      breath,
each one a shuddering
terror, a
prophecy of when you won't be able,
the dark descending
spirit ascending,
as it floats from the skin of your shell
to that moment when breath no longer matters
      anymore.

Me stupid

When me come out weak thin starve
four pound small by measurement,
say me owl-eyed, silent, say me carve
in color cocoa, say day by day me sent
them marvel still me live.
Not till later school, me nine,
it defect show, they say 'count of no give
answer like they others shine,
me stupid, bullied dirt thrown, hit
then rape in playground, then times more,
and more cuz of me no fit
for better say they, boy hitch jeans me too sore
walk weep by me lone, me mamma high
me papa gone. Fourteen now and baby nigh,

belly-big, me eat, want feed she, and when me lie
in bed me whisper to she, sing, me sigh
how she gon be so pretty, yes, have faculties
read write be smart not be deaf like me.

I live in my body like a suitcase

I live in my body like a suitcase
that I carry around, knocking on my knees.
It's battered now, beat up,
the corners crushed and the
fine leather scuffed and scarred.
The dull stuffing shows through in places,
but I clutch it tight,
lest someone snatch it off.

I think of myself (who hides inside)
as dazzling, a shining
essence and also maybe twenty-five—
I'm shocked when the mirror
reflects my suitcase back instead.
But still it's *mine*.
No one else can have my case.

My suitcase has been loved
by others too. Other
hands have polished its brass locks,
run tender fingers along the straps
and ridges of its fine design.
Others have murmured how beautiful
my suitcase is.

But someday, in a while,
I'll set it on the floor,
flip up the locks,
and pull myself out like laundry on the line,
white shirt flapping in the wind.

My suitcase will be buried in the dump
or burned, grey smoke from chimneys
built especially for that purpose.
I think I won't regret the loss.
I'm told you can always lease another
if you wish.

The meaning of life

Asked the meaning of life,
The Buddha
Held up a flower. . .
       And one monk smiled.

I see it as an iris
Small as wild things often are
A brave and violent blue
Licked by a
       yellow tongue.

No others
In the gathered crowd
Quite got it.
What? They whispered.
Huh? and *What's that
      supposed to mean?*

The iris blinked
Its blue-and-yellow
      eye and smiled.

I'm not sure I remember the story right,
But wasn't there a test
To see which monk
Had reached enlightenment,
Would wear the Buddha's mantle
When he passed along?

I think the one who smiled,
Wasn't he the lowly kitchen-boy?

Stand guard against your thoughts

I am a gazelle chewing
the green cud of contentment,
legs folded under me relaxed
and yet aware it's dangerous
when a lioness lurks in the brush
watching, tawny;
see her tail tip flick
her leap;
And in a flash

I'm on my feet and fleeing
in great bounds across the brown savannah
the high bronze grass

knowing it is hopeless—no escape—

I'm felled, feet thrashing at
remembrances of breathing in
your body scent
your weight on mine, your smile
your hands which smooth the hips
of someone other now, kiss other lips,
skin trembling, shuddering, heat high,
and my body quivering before the coming
thought. I turn to face
the lioness, the way she crouches
the way she tucks her chin, eyes

glittering
before she pounces
breaks my back
with loss.

Gunfight

So he's a gun owner and when he
Asked me to lunch I said
Hey, there's a march Sunday against
Gun violence, wanna go?
And he thought he hadn't heard right.
He said, What? And then he mumbled No,
I'll pass. I don't believe in that.
So I said, don't believe in what? Gun safety?
No one's in favor of killing little children
With guns, no one's in favor of that.
He said, Who's going to be there?
And I said I didn't know but imagine it
Would be people against shooting kids,
Since another guy shot up another school today
And killed a dozen more, and he said he
Bet the NRA would not attend and
I agreed, and he said
He was a member of the NRA and therefore
Wouldn't go, no.
So that's how I got out of going to lunch
With a guy I had no interest in.

Trying on clothes

When you come to think about it,
It's stories we're trying on
All the time and taking off
Like clothes in the closet or Macy's dressing room.
We plunk down dollars for the daily news
Or tune to tales on Fox or NPR,
And those are true events, or as true as stories get
When they have to have sewn seams,
Frills and finished hem.
When we grow bored
We read a novel or biography
Or else indulge in gossip,
Which is another word for tattletales
About our friends or enemies; and finally
We tug over our heads sometimes
The tales we tell ourselves,
The sweater of *I'm Not Enough*,
Which looks pretty good on you, I'd say,
Then reconsider, no,
Not Good Enough, and change it for the
Turtleneck of Downright Failure, Never
Amount to a Hill of Beans,
Told You So,
Fake, fraud, passé.

You twirl before the mirror, head cocked,
Assessing how the skirt swishes
Sexy at the knee, considering how
This one's pretty good except
I'm A Victim hangs on a hook nearby
All pleats and ruffles, tempting, and
Here's a winter coat untried so far, so
On with that one too: *Too Late, Too Old, Washed up.*
It's sorta okay, but you want to
Go back to the turtleneck
That felt so warm and comfy, an old friend:
Failure, Hill of Beans, Told You So, You Fake:
That's a story you can get real mileage from.

Climbing Mount Robert, Alaska

John asked me
As I set out to climb Mount Robert
"Where do you get your energy?"
I laughed his curiosity aside,

But stepping out
              And upward
    Light of heart
              And joyful in my breath,
Knees like scissors
Closing strong at each upswinging stride
The answer quivered in the spruce-green air,
It sang upon my eagle skin.

As the traveler by night
Quickens his step at the home light's prick,
As the lover leaps up
At sight of her beloved
(Exhaustion dropped)
                 To race into his arms,
So I
Rejoicing climb.
I step upon the
              Flames of His beneficence
And sink in worship
Before red yellow blue pink
Flowing from the face of rocks.
    They scrawl His name across the sky
         My God!
I cry
         My God!
And weep the silver ribbons
Pouring down green mountain slopes,
                 Cascades,
To find myself once more
Held in the arms
Of that deep Suchness
              Love.

June cornflowers

All across the country
The cornflowers bloom in the tall grasses
Along the sides of roads
While cars, trucks, trailers, vans, and
Rolling eighteen-wheeler fortresses
Thunder past, blow dirt
And pebbled asphalt, toss gravel high onto the edge
Where the weeds burst forth wild and cheeky,
Exuberant, defiant, demanding place.
They clutch with barren fingerholds at stones, dry dust
Uplifting toward the light.
You find them
Massachusetts to New Mexico,
Modest in their self-effacing sovereignty,
While all around crowded in lusher loam bloom
Queen Anne's lace and tiger lilies fierce as sunset,
White daisies, cosmos, clover, pink alfalfa.
Only the lovely blue chicory stands apart, plucky
And shivering
Like snippets from the hems of angels' gowns
Scattered in the stones.

You can have your summer romance

You can have your summer romance or
The heady love affair
With its half-life as the poet says of two years
But I'll take the hour that summer when
Ten-year-old Adelaide lay beside me
On the black-and-white cushions of the carriage house
Couch, and we watched a movie of
Tuck Everlasting
Because she had just finished
The book and wanted to share it with me;
And I remember the way she reached out at a
Certain point as we lay stretched out,
The computer on her lap,
The way she glanced up at me with her owl eyes,
Tucked her arm behind me and pulled my head to hers
So that it rested on her little shoulder.
She pulled me to her, hugging with both hands tight,
And I wound my arms round her. We lay like that, rejoicing,
Comfortable with the images flickering in the dark,
And it is her growing body I feel beside me. Was I ever so small,
So open,
So present to the moment,
So ready to leap
To the next stage?

The road less traveled on a snowy night
(with apologies to Robert Frost)

When he stopped in the snowy woods,
Pausing to look at the glittering trees encased in ice
Like jewels in the velvet box of a salt gray sky,
The snow sifting pastern-deep
And the sledge runners suddenly silent; having stopped
His horse at the fork in the track
(its hot breath foaming in the air,
And don't forget the shake of its head,
The impatient jingle of reins and tack),
He took, he says, the road less traveled by,
Which one teacher of mine opined
Was a metaphor of death
And another claimed was life,
Or choosing what was right for him, society be damned,
And probably family responsibilities and friendships too.

But I keep thinking of the horse
And how it would have bucked and swerved
And shied, refusing that narrow snow-packed path,
Because horses know which way leads home.
And in the dusk of that late evening the pony
Would have had enough of woods in snow
And cold. It wanted its warm stable
With its thick bed of knee-deep straw;
The Dutch doors closed against the night,
And the sweet smell of other horses rising from the stalls nearby.
It would have fought for its head, ears pinned,
In knowledge of those woods and which way to go,
And it's not by the less travelled route.
I think the owner in his sleigh might have had a tough time of it,
Whipping the pony to trot that trackless way
(The red sun bleeding through the branches)
Especially if he had a long way to go that night,

Unless it led, a shortcut,
To the stone gateposts of his farm.
Which would explain why he'd turned off the main road in the first place,
Not to mention why the pony uncomplaining
Pulled the hill. He was heaving up his own driveway
Less trafficked than the public road
Just heading home.

In the silence of sleeping

At night
In the silence of sleeping
She drifts from bed to bed
So many cots, so many wounded hearts
Or legs, arms, eyes, ears, parts.

She's just a metaphor (bear with me)
Pale as breath
A thought, a dream, an inspiration,
Faint as fantasy.

Not real, you say, despite the glory blinding
You; shivering shadow slivers

Seeming nothingness.
She ought to fade, to disappear.
But see her cover a forehead with one soothing hand,
Smile, let fall a tear of pity
On that hurt, just there.

They are so young, so brave,
So old, so mangled, strangled by misplaced perception.

How hard it is to be a human
And bear in silence,
Patient as a dog or ox,
Loss piled on loss.
How hard to be a human
And not hear how much we're loved, or
        (shh)
It's going to be all right,
Different tomorrow, interesting, a challenge,
And how rich is life, how sweet,

How hard when you don't know
That even
The black wall impenetrable
That you cannot feel or scratch
Your fingernails on
Is merely more illusion
As evidenced by the phantom singing here
Silver moon-music
Swelling your heart unreasonably
With joy.

Granddaughters

Well, here's the thing.
They're so new, don't you see,
Their skin woven of fine silk and eyes like
The eyes of antelopes, wide, curious,
And often a little wary of what's about
To come, which is only
Right given the cuffs Life's dealing out
To us all the time—the back of the hand
To you, sir, who think you know
The road. They know they don't know any of the roads,
Which is why the feel of
That little hand reaching up to yours
As you walk, tiny
Fingers holding on, holding on,
Safe inside your broad, flat palm
Catches in your throat and tugs
The kite strings of your twisting heart
High into the soaring sky.

When I Was a Leaf

When I was a leaf
uncurling from the cocoon of my green sheath
my fetal wings unfolding,
it was joyous, exuberant,
the music crashing like breakers against
the sea walls, and later, riding the winds,
held tight by the mother of my tree,
our little paws clapping with delight—
I didn't think it could get any better
ever, each
mouth lifted to the drenching rains,
and then the golden burst of final joy
clad in gold burnt umber red
and all of us shouting screaming shrieking
LOOKIT ME
Before I jump. Oh,
even the downward drift was
delirious, twirling gyroscopic dizzying
in this final venture when I get to sleep,
decay, shed skin, to molt into the mud,
lie mute in memory

Sophy Burnham has written novels, films, plays, journalism, nonfiction, short stories, essays and articles. Her works are translated into 26 languages. Three of her books made the *New York Times* and other bestseller lists. She is best known for writing on mysticism, including *A Book of Angels, The Ecstatic Journey,* and *The Treasure of Montségur*. Her favorite award is "Daughter of Mark Twain."

Working closely with famed Broadway producer, Roger Stevens, she served for five years as Executive Director of the John F. Kennedy Fund for New American Plays, giving money to theaters to produce new plays and to playwrights to write them.

Her play *Prometheus* (an adaptation of the Aeschylus fragment with a new conclusion) was produced at the Studio Theatre in Washington, DC. Her award-winning play *Penelope* (the story of the Odyssey from Penelope's point of view) was staged most recently at American University.

She has appeared on scores of TV and radio shows. She lives in Washington, D. C. and Northampton, MA.

www.Sophyburnham.com

www.ingramcontent.com/pod-product-compliance
Lightning Source LLC
LaVergne TN
LVHW041327080426
835513LV00008B/619